New Hues

and

Past Tales

a collection of poems

Edmond Bruneau

ISBN: 978-1-936769-91-9
Library of Congress Control Number: 2016910210

Cover Design: Edmond Bruneau
Illustration: Lisa Zador

For Donna –
whose continual
encouragement
made this book happen.

FORWARD

When I was young, I wrote poems all the time. Then, for whatever reason, I quit. Perhaps since I was a commercial writer for so many years, I didn't have anything left in the tank for myself after writing for others.

I began attending a weekly poetry workshop at the beginning of 2015 to learn, after all those years, if I still had any sort of poetry mojo. In addition, I wanted to see if I would still enjoy the process. The answer was a resounding YES!

A special thanks to Lisa Conger, who leads the local poetry workshop with enthusiasm and inspiration, as well as the rest of the class participants for their helpful support.

This collection of poetry covers many subjects and can be humorous, sad, thoughtful or silly. My hope is, you as the reader will enjoy them as much as I did writing them.

– Edmond Bruneau

TABLE OF CONTENTS

Things to Put in my Pocket

Before I die, I'll take
a few things from my closet.
Sneak them along as I ascend,
tuck them into my soul pocket.

First and foremost I will take
the love I've given and gotten –
packed and folded carefully,
never to be forgotten.

The saturation of a sunset.
Laughter of a child.
A tender kiss, a runaway tear,
my imagination running wild.

Smell of frying bacon.
Warmth of a campfire.
A raven's call, a seagull's squall,
my insatiable desire.

I want to take the music.
I want to take the dance.
I want to bundle up it all
than leave it left for chance.

Don't want to leave mistakes behind
or the lessons that I've learned.
I will carry them with me,
and bring them back when I return.

Get it Right this Time

Re-entry in 1953.
Another chance to shine.
Everything new
surrounds you.
Get it right this time.

Photos and first memories.
Ektachrome, Black & White.
Few things familiar
from former formulation.
Searching for the light.

Here to learn. Here to live.
Who, what, when and how.
Most people
spend a lifetime
trying to figure it out.

No roadmap. No GPS.
It's that way by design.
Storms and struggle,
pieces to the puzzle.
Get it right this time.

Maybe a major overhaul
or just a simple fine tuning.
Move forward, not back.
Look ahead, not behind.
Progress is resuming.

Maybe I'll be kinder.
Better listener. Better friend.
Time for those
less fortunate.
Time that's tough to spend.

People talk evolution,
a monkey to a man.
Small steps toward
enhancements
advances and expands.

Re-entry since 1953.
Keep all of it in mind.
Another opportunity
to move ahead.
Get it right this time.

Mini Miracles

A stranger's smile.
An encouraging word.
Novocain.
Laughter.
A cats purr.
Coltrane.
Bird songs.
Starfish.
Hope.
Dental Floss.
Holding hands.
Heliotrope.
Popsicles.
Dreams.
Marching bands.
Toilet paper.
Butterflies.
Soap.
Hugs.
Microwave ovens.
Memories.
Slumber.
Watermelon.
Screw cap wine.
Wheels.
Bacon.
Fingernail clippers.
Sand castles.
DVRs.
Chocolate raisins.
Bananas.
Beer.

Saint Chicago

A man rushed past me,
held open the door for
an invisible old woman
and helped her out to her car.
A smile was his reward.
I could see her now.

I followed him to the street
filled with shrieks of saxophone.
He stopped for a moment
and put five dollars in an invisible hat,
suddenly appearing
next to the street musician.

Then he walked over
to an invisible soul
with a cardboard sign,
talked with him a bit
about the weather, laughed
and bought him a hot dog.

I wondered what
secret of vision that man has –
to see beyond the
city life camouflage.
Some of us
barely see with our eyes
while others
see more with their hearts.

I wanted to buy him a hotdog, too.
As a humble human thank you.
But I didn't.

I'll Tell You What Happens

If you already knew
what would happen today,
would you do it anyway?

Would you put a bet on the horses
if positively a sure thing?
Pick up the phone and say hello
before it had a chance to ring?

Anticipate all the accidents
and be the one who knows
who would or would not live?
Follow the script or just adlib?

Would you make the same mistakes
that are waiting for you to make?
Would you say the words over again
and cause the same heartache?

Will your dreams seem like a replay
when you know what will occur next?
When the mystery's gone and you go along
will you ever be perplexed?

No longer an adventure.
Never a surprise.
Results always predictable
no matter how many tries.

If you knew the future
do you think you could change it?
Make it better than the original –
revamp and rearrange it?

We have the power to change things now
without knowledge of the outcome.
The future is actually already here
and it's live instead of a rerun.

Don't need to see tomorrow
before today falls to abandon.
If you feel your fate is important to know,
I'll tell you what happens.

Fireflies of Icarus

A place beyond our atmosphere –
A place that knows no bounds.
A place where absence abides frontier.
A place where space surrounds.

It was John Glenn
who first saw them –
a mirage of marvelous mirth –
fireflies from the capsule window
a century from earth.

The Fireflies of Icarus swarmed
the solitary schooner of space.
A puzzlement of particles.
Cosmic chagrin embraced.

The slide rules were stumped.
NASA's best were bewildered.
What magical enchantment exists
beyond our own earthward?

Another flight, another time,
Scott Carpenter saw them again.
Outside the Aurora 7 when
reconciliation would rescind.

Ice particles, not wings of wax,
the genesis of these flies.
The sleuth had solved the mystery.
Now no longer a solar surprise.

Farewell Fireflies of Icarus.
Farewell the celestial saga
of a lifeform's galactic infinity
into zilch, nothing and nada.

First Kiss

I remember the day of my first kiss.
Morning Kindergarten. Still Summer.
Riding home on the bus at noon with
the sun glaring through the windows –
warming the plum vinyl seats,
magically softening them for sitting.

I sat next to you, Jenny.
A neighbor girl. A twin.
Whose sister Becky attended the other class
and sat with another neighbor up front.
I sat next to you and held your hand.
We had many stops to go
before the bus dropped us off at our homes.

I thought you were beautiful.
A brunette with a pixie cut.
With a smile that let me know
sitting close to you was welcome.
There was a softness about you, a shyness.
I was suspended in that moment of time until
a voice came from the older boys behind us.

"Is this your girlfriend?" one of them asked.
The happy five year old smiled,
"Yes, she is, I guess."
"Then you gotta kiss her!" another commanded.
"Kiss her! Kiss her! Kiss her!" they taunted
together. So I did. And she didn't resist.
"Again!" they all cried. *"Again!"*
And we kissed a dozen times more, before the
snickering and laughter of the others made us
both feel guilty. And judged. And wrong.

Said goodbye when her stop came, sheepishly.
The hoot and hollers from the back of the bus
finally quieted.
And I pondered if I was to be punished upon
arriving home.
But there was no mention of it.
From me or my family.
I felt ashamed and didn't understand why.

The next day I was hoping
to see Jenny at school. She was absent.
I felt like I might have caused it.
"Where's your GIRLfriend?" the boys on the bus
bellowed.
"She is sick today," Becky told them.
"You'll probably get her cold," one said to me.
"After all, you KISSED her!"

Sometimes it's just a little thing
that can cause a trama.
And for a little boy, naivety alone is adequate.
Jenny was absent for the rest of the week.
When she returned, she avoided me.
And never sat alone on the bus home again.

I remember my first kiss, with Jenny.
Forced. Subject to ridicule. Mortified.
It would be many more years
before I would again kiss a girl starry-eyed.

Summer in Color

In June of
my seventh year,
our black and white
TV went down.

Gone were my
morning cartoons
and afternoon
kid shows.

Without my
familiar friend,
I was bored.
Lincoln Logs
and Tinkertoys
only amused
so long.

My mother
said go outside.
There was
weeding in the garden.

A row was assigned
and I'd put weeds
in a bucket.
I was not very
good at it.

"By the roots,"
my mother
commanded.
Yet, much of
what I pulled
let the roots remain.

"Dig some worms,"
she suggested.
And as I dug
a shovel into the
rich garden soil,
I found worms. Pill bugs.
And speckled rocks.

Then I discovered
a bone – or rather
a small skull.
I showed my mother
and we were both
mystified for a moment.
*"You dug where
we bury cats,"* she explained.

I kept the skull
for a while –
even though it
creeped me out.
Then went off
to capture
grasshoppers
in a jar.

Next day,
I was
smart enough
to go outside
without
being told.
Explore
the creek,
the woods,
the field.
And avoid
gardening
at all costs.

In June of
my seventh year,
our black and white
TV went down.
My father had
pulled a tube –
to make me see
the summer
in color.

Grandmother's Supper

It was a small kitchen,
my grandmother's.
Somehow, though
she nimbly navigated
fried chicken, mashed taters
and vegetable greens
with ease.
Gravy from the drippings.
Bread rolls
baking in the oven.
All served piping hot
on platters and in bowls –
supper for the waiting hungry.
Pumpkin pie's undeniable aroma
drifts into the dining area and
reminds us to save
room for dessert.
Dirty pans and dishes
in the small country sink –
testament to
kindred gatherings,
chipped plates and all.
As each piece is washed
rinsed and dried,
the sounds, the smells,
the tastes of her
inconspicuous efforts
remain unscathed.

High as a Kite

Sail my soul into the air
with a warm soft breeze.
Let me fly high as a kite –
shed ballast from my disease.

Tie a tail of knotted cloth.
Steady my stance to soar.
Let me fly high as a kite –
and feel like I did before.

Give me line. Let me climb
above the field below.
Let me fly high as a kite –
escape the world I know.

Mollify my yearn to fly.
Give me gossamer wings.
Let me fly high as a kite –
gently unwind my string.

Watch me rise onto the stars.
Become one of them instead.
Let me fly high as a kite –
depart the burden of my bed.

Don't bring me back. Let me ascend.
Cut the string that keeps me here.
Let me fly high as a kite –
and abandon this atmosphere.

Carnival Glass

At the carnival,
barkers bellow
games so easy
a child could do it.
They lie, by the way.

A booth sells
caramel apples
on popsicle sticks.
The standard in
reverse dentistry.

The bearded lady
proudly sashays
her flamboyant gown –
a gasp of feminine flair
from an ape-like angel.

The Fun House
frightens even
the strong of heart,
accomplishing
everything but fun.

A seat on the
Ferris Wheel
ascends toward a
bird's-eye view of
the masquerade below.

A little boy plays Bingo
with his last quarter and wins.
His prize – a shimmering
purple and blue vase
he takes home to his mother.

Broken Wing

Something is broken.
Favorite toy gets put away.
Dish dropped in garbage.
Water heater all washed-up.
Printer needs a cartridge.

Something is broken.
Road rife with potholes.
Traffic grinds to halt.
Bridge closed for repair.
Government's in default.

Something is broken.
Can't attain consensus.
Don't see eye to eye.
Rising river floods.
Clamor clouds the sky.

Something is broken.
Forgot how the TV works.
Toaster burnt the bread.
Can't drive the car no more.
Newspaper's barely read.

Something is broken.
King without his queen.
Nothing left to conquer.
Still sings with a broken wing.
Ascends to fly no longer.

No Longer Zeus

Through my eyes
I always thought
of my Dad as young.

Vibrant. Strong.
Clear-eyed and alive.
Straight black hair
like a movie star –
Always combed
with a perfect wave.
Preserved like a magazine ad
for Vaseline Hair Tonic.

But something changed when
my folks once came to visit.
Wire rim glasses
made him look older.
There were new wrinkles
when he laughed.
His thinning midnight mane
seemed to have turned
to dusk overnight.

Suddenly I realized
my vision of him
had altered as well.
Gone was the icon
I had held as gospel
for my forty-six years.

Now in its place –
an aging god.
Vulnerable in battle.
Chinks in his armor.
Still willing to
come to my aid
as if
summer had never
turned to fall at all.

My father,
no longer Zeus –
but a mortal man
who gets wet
when it rains.

I said farewell
to the temple Olympus
and held him even closer.
The days of wear
finally found my heart
when my dear young Dad
got older.

Hoist Anchor

Let my heart
sail past the shoal –
avoid the shallow sediment.
Navigate into waters deep
to shirk the silt and sentiment.

Fathom my love
as it collects at the mouth –
free from waves and wakes.
Kiss me long. Kiss me deep.
Give as well as take.

Dredge my soul,
scoop out your spot
as we embark our voyage.
Let us depart safe harbor –
neither of us hostage.

Captain my course,
maneuver the helm,
steer us toward our destiny.
Cast out our frets and past regrets –
smooth waters for our journey.

Common Bond

Bashful buds
burst into blossom.
New leaves
cheer them on
like a crowd at a marathon.

Robins capture worms
from fresh cut lawn –
then back to nest.
Hungry mouths
await to digest.

Scents. Sounds. Insights robust –
awakening Spring blooms within us.
Renewal. Awakening. Reflection.
Seeds of self begin to sprout –
personal growth emerging out.

Sunshine nourishes longer days –
triumphs over winter grey.
What surrounds us is our nature, too.
New life. New warmth. New color.
A common bond to be discovered.

Sally, My Collie

I was seven the summer
with the halo 'round the sun.
My dog Sally had been chasin' chickens.
And eating chicken feed,
which made her eyes blood red.
It was Grandpa's chicken farm
across the field. Actually, it
was an egg farm that used
chickens as the middle man – *err bird*.
This time it was serious misbehavior.
Grandpa told Dad he would
shoot that dog next time
he caught her in the act.
Not long after, Sally started
roaming with a pack of
neighborhood dogs at night,
chasing some of the calves.
Grandma said it was the
chicken feed Sally ate that
made her do such crazy things.
The phone rang, it was Grandpa
talking to Dad. After that,
Mom and Dad spoke solemnly,
quietly, soberly, softly.
I couldn't quite make out the words.
Somehow, though, I knew
Sally was going away.

Next morning after breakfast
I heard the John Deere out in the field,
climbed under the fence,
ran to the tractor, and got hoisted up
on Grandpa's lap. *"You steer,"* he said.
I pulled on the levers that
made the tractor go right or left.
*"Someday you'll see the year 2000.
I won't, but you will."* I hadn't thought
about the year 2000 before. I looked
around at the large field of wild oats and
pondered the idea of Grandpa dying.
I hadn't thought about that before, either.
There was no talk of Sally from that point on.
That was the day I grew up a little bit.

Wide Awake, 3am

Sleep was welcome
as I shut my eyes.
Soon, as the rain
began sounding
like radio static,
I turned the volume down,
entering a world
of restful slumber.
Dark. Quiet. Serene.
And then, suddenly awake.
3:00am, the clock declared.
Too early. Too black.
Closed my eyelids tighter,
pretending it never happened.
A horse whinnies.
The house creaks.
Leaves rustle.
All the sounds
sleep circumvents –
amplified
in the darkness.
Why did you abandon me,
my drowsy friend?
Don't leave me here, alone.
Come back.
Come back and rescue me
from my thoughts and fears
and regrets.
The horse whinnies again.
Maybe it's laughter
at the poor souls
roused from their
nocturnal tranquility.
Just a few more hours, I beg.
Sometimes sleep has no mercy.

Will Work for Food

The cardboard sign read
HUNGRY – WILL WORK FOR FOOD
but it actually looked as if
he could lose a few pounds.
Would he really work for food?
Or is he content
grabbing the five
and ten dollar bills
from the guilty
and the generous?
I would have no problem
buying him a meal
at the café
after he rakes my leaves.
Or cleans my gutters.
I would love to
know his story.
We could chat while
he enjoyed today's
blue plate special.
Maybe he was
a refugee from Katrina
and lost it all in the storm.
Maybe he once
had a family and a job
but it all disappeared
with his gambling addiction.
But that's not how it works, is it?
I'm not going to share conversation
over a blue plate special.
And he's not going to
rake my leaves.
But he'll take my five,
tuck it away
and put it toward
a bottle of Thunderbird.
In a sad, sick way
we both feel a little better.

The World Grows Up Around Me

Drove past where I grew up.
The homestead gone, as are the
chickens, cows, pigs and ducks.
New homes starting at $800,000
reads the sign.
I can still remember the half mile hike
across the field to visit my grandparents.
I flew kites in that field. Explored nature
down at the creek. Picked blackcaps
from a secret spot in the woods.
I don't recognize it any longer.

I'm still the same person inside
who stood in the rain with my lunchbox
waiting for the school bus.
The world grew up around me.
The radio station I worked at
changed its name and call letters.
The world's largest electronic sign
manufacturer gave me five years
before it crept to its demise.
Raised two kids. Now grown.
They grew up around me.

I look in the mirror and see a resemblance
of the boy I was and the man I've become.
My dark hair has grown to grey.
When you are on the carrousel,
everyone else sharing a ride looks fine
as the world blurs by.
A French author once wrote,
"the more things change,
the more they stay the same"
I believe he was mistaken.
Everything changes.
And nothing stays the same.
Even me.

10:16pm on Dearborn

Not a pleasant person
to encounter on this night –
a repulsive odor
dressed in abhorrent rags –
feigning for a fight.
My leftover box of pizza
altered the altercation
to be a little more polite.
To say it was consumed
would actually be contrite.
Let's just say
this person had
a raucous appetite.
After that, a little smile
grew to a sassy smirk.
"Sorry," the person said
"for being such a jerk."
When the hand reached inside
a duffle bag,
it put me on alert.
"Something for you"
said the tattered tramp –
a fez fit for a Turk.
*"Thanks for being so kind,
I do my own needlework."*

Mom's Basket

There's a basket
in the kitchen
Mom made for me.
I can imagine her
weaving pine needles
gingerly.
Slowly forming
a bowl with
intricate patterns
and a practical handle.

Every time I see it,
I'm reminded of
her natural
artistic ability.
Her profuse patience.
Her love of
creating beauty
with her hands.

She carved me
an original Santa
every Christmas
for nineteen years
until arthritis
crippled her craft.

Now that she's gone
and I'm older,
those precious gifts –
materialized
from her muse –
touch me in a way
no *"store bought"*
ever could.

She is still with me
in every woven strand –
in every whittle and chisel.
Seeds of her soul
she secretly left behind.

Pal

When our garden was in full glory,
we'd throw green over the fence
for the cows to eat. Lettuce leaves,
corn stalks, even buckets of weeds
freshly plucked. The cows would
notice the new treats quickly.
In minutes, a dozen or so Herefords
were feasting on the foliage.

As kids, we loved to
feed the cows by hand.
One cow in particular would
run right over anytime it
saw us near the barbed-wire fence.
My sister would grab some tall grass
and pet the gentle cow's white curls
on it's forehead. She named it *"Pal."*
Over the course of the summer,
she would call to Pal and
it came runnin' – ready for a
little scratchin' and a tasty tidbit.
She loved Pal.

Late Fall, our family had a tradition –
Steaks at Grandma & Grandpa's place
right after the butcher was done.
There were four of us at the kid's table.
I waited until her meat was almost gone.
"Enjoy your steak?" I asked my sis.
"Yes," she replied, *"it was really good."*
"Well, Pal was a good cow!" I exclaimed!
Took her a moment to connect the dots.
Her innocent smile vanished.

When I think back, it's hard to excuse
my childish behavior. Except I
was a child as well, be it an older one.
I should have let her figure it out herself
when Pal no longer came to her call.
I got no joy from her sadness.
Pal gave me a lesson to learn, too.

I Will Wait

They say
waiting for a cause
without a cure
is time spent
on futility –
the toughest to endure.

But to wait no more
abandons hope,
silences prayers
and shuts the door
for one who cares.

I am the light
at the end
of a tunnel –
the smile
when you awake.
Damn the word
"impossible" –
stealing when
nothing's left to take.

The definition
of a miracle
is an act
against the odds.
And waiting
for one
isn't madness –
it's a belief
there is a God.

Waiting then
is never wrong
no matter what they say –
no matter when or how or why –
no matter what gets in the way,
I will wait.
I will wait.
I will wait for you and pray

Raven's Call

Black
bird
oversees
from treetop.
Watches.
Listens.
Awaits.
He is a spirit,
this one.
A presence.
Guided by senses
stronger
than the wind.
Guided by ribbons
that tie us all
together.
He needs
to be here
at this moment.
Not for
himself,
but for
appearance
by other eyes
and other hearts.
A symbol.
A totem.
A sign.
A puzzle piece
of the universe
we're not meant
to understand.
Yet, he remains
perched on treetop,
calling out to those
meant to hear.
Representing
a voice
beyond heaven.
A call for change.
A call for truth.
A call for cause.

Redmond in the Rain

There's one reason why the
western side of Washington State
is so damn green.
Rain.
Summer peeks out late June
and retires late September –
then the season of wet and gray
for nearly nine months.
I remember as a kid
waiting outside with my lunchbox
for the school bus to arrive.
In the rain.
I was envious of bus stops where
someone had built a shelter
and the kids climbed
on the bus happy.
And dry.
Recess meant
leaving the cozy classroom –
tetherball and foursquare
in the blacktop puddles.
Waiting for the bell to ring
to hang up my soaked coat.
Damp, like my spirit.
One day my family
took a trip to the
eastern side of Washington.
We visited three hydroelectric dams
in blue sky and sunshine.
And had a picnic.
When we drove back
my father turned the
windshield wipers on
as we headed home over the pass.
When I got old enough
to depart my soggy nest
and leave the constant grey days
of precipitation behind.
I did.
Smiling.

A Good Day for Fishin'

The homemade boat hits the shore with a hiss
as it slides from sand into lake.
It was my Uncle's boat,
a pram of planks with plywood bottom.
Heavy, even in water, coming up
within an inch of the top
when three of us rode inside.

My Uncle took the oars. It was raining –
pouring actually.
He laughed and claimed
it was a good day for fishin'.
For Uncle Don, it was always
a good day for fishin',
no matter what the weather.

We rowed to his favorite spot.
Between a windmill on one side
and abandoned truck on the other.
My father threw out the first anchor,
a rusty rectangular pail of cement.
Don eased the other into the water gently,
then reaching for the mason jar
of eggshells and chum,
tossing it out with a spoon
as if he was feeding pigeons.

I made noise, like young boys do,
filling the muffled nature of the lake
with nervous questions and comments.
My father told me to be quiet,
I would scare the fish.
They both spoke softly, just above a whisper,
assembling three-part split bamboo poles
with simple flat reels and four pound test line.
Using half pound leader,
my father doublehooked
one with worm, one with salmon egg.
He stripped out some line, elegantly tossed it
into the lake and handled me the pole.

The worm and the egg floated on the water
and slowly, very slowly sank deeper
until disappearing in the depths.
"What do we do now?" I asked
in my 'quiet as possible' voice.
"We wait," my father said.
"And watch the line."
The line was all curly from pole to the water.
We waited. I could hear other people talking
from boats nearby.
But both men in ours sat hushed and still,
like a cat waiting to pounce on a mouse.
Suddenly, I saw Don's line twitch tight.
He let it jerk two or three times
then whipped his long pole up into the air.
He laughed again and said,
"Got him, the little rascal."
It was a moment to talk, as the fish
was netted into the boat. He showed me
how big it was and banged its head
with a old screwdriver so it wouldn't suffer.
And we were back to quiet once again.

We all caught fish that day.
I lost more than I landed.
Once, Don had two fish on at the same time.
He laughed at the absurdity of it all,
avoiding anchor ropes
and safely landing them both in the boat.
It was a bonding time, two men and a boy.
The test of patience.
The thrill of fish on the line.
The heartbreak of a lost catch.
The pride of providing for the family meal.

We rowed back silently to shore,
meeting others who wondered how we did.
"Alright, I guess," my father would answer.
And I never knew if he chose
not to boast or brag,
or simply avoided
sharing the secret spot.

Shipwrecked

Shipwrecked in the Caribbean.
Sabotaged from the sea.
Victim of pirate plunder.
No where else to flee.

No escape. Must face the day.
Realize the reality.
Moment of truth. Unveil the flaws.
Abandon my fantasy.

You broke my heart this one last time.
Such misbehavior I allowed –
overlooked, not unperceived.
It really gnaws at me now.

But it is not I who needs rescue.
Or a map to arrange retreat.
Memories will be a memory.
Life is bittersweet.

I deserve better in my paradise.
Resolution, my reward.
You're no longer in my rear view.
Recovering. Moving forward.

Over Your Head

Shingle by shingle,
one by one,
overlap every piece
until it's finally done.
It's how you build
a shelter.
It's how you build
a shield.
It's how you build protection
for a heart not fully healed.
Armor from the elements.
Safeguard from saboteurs.
Break free beyond
hamper and hindrance –
unless you make them yours.

Appomattox Awaits

Raise the
white flag.
I will
argue
no longer.
Too many
losses
left me
weaker,
not stronger.

I was
always
taught to
battle on.
Fight the
good fight.
Bring
darkness
to dawn.

But I am
weary of
the war.
Tired of
gore.
Sick of
keeping score.
Finished with my
formidable foe.

Let us
raise a
glass of wine
and toast
to our
new truce.
Cease fire
on our
front lines.
Amnesty
from abuse.

It may
be called
surrender,
but there's
more to it
than that.
Isn't peace
a better
resolve?
Concession
better than
combat?

Let our
wounds
heal time,
our grief
no longer
grate.
Put the
past
behind us
now.
Appomattox
awaits.

When Dreams Come True

I knew something like this would happen.
I dreamt it years ago.
When we were first going out
and getting to know each other better.
It came to me in a dream
that we would marry
but
you would die young. Before me.
I didn't tell you then because
it was lousy date conversation.
And I thought I was secretly prepared
to face the worst when it happened.
At thirty-six you had dozens
of doctor visits.
Seemed it took forever to discover
your appendix had to go.
After the operation,
I found you in the early morning,
on a hospital lower floor,
covered in a light sheet
in a quiet dark room, all alone.
You were shivering and I found you a blanket.
I thought we might have cheated it.
But then, at 53,
a week after Dean's September wedding,
I dropped you off at urgent care
to get your annoying cough examined,
while I drove off and gassed up the car.
I returned and you were still in the exam room.
Finally, you came out and said
you think there's something wrong
because everyone was whispering.
I said don't worry,
it's probably your imagination.
But it wasn't.
Your lung had collapsed. And you had cancer.
You left me at 55. Older than I thought you'd be
from my dream those years ago.
But younger than you should have been.
I don't know why it was foretold.

Sometimes I hate it when dreams come true.

Seed of Inspiration

A song on the car radio.
A little child's smile.
A note from a long lost friend.
A sadness that stays awhile.
A tear upon your pillow –
the kindle of the light.
Inspiration – a delicate dame
who plays with dynamite.

Sometimes a glimmer of thought.
Sometimes a whisper.
Sometimes you welcome her in.
Sometimes you resist her.
Sometimes a taste, a smell,
yields a vision to remember.
Inspiration – a fickle flame
fueled by tinder tender.

She arrives in a fleeting moment.
Perhaps even in a dream.
Elusively intangible.
A minnow in a stream.
A notion may emerge –
nursed from its natal nest.
Inspiration – a gift to ascertain
how its beauty's been beset.

Just as suddenly then, she's gone.
Left to capture her lingering scent.
Her temporary tarriance –
wondering where she went.
Leaving behind an offering –
beggars banquet bestowed.
Inspiration – from whence she came
a seed for one to sow.

Hard Knocks Equinox

I'm a wanderer. A vagabond.
A traveling tumbleweed.
Some banter with the barkeep
who says, "I'm a dying breed."
Can't stay in a place too long
or start to turn to seed.
A backpack and a few greenbacks
are really all I need.
But I've learned the hard way
to go south when days grow short.
Below the Mason-Dixon,
where I must transport –
to drink December margaritas
and tease tourists, just for sport.
Come March, days grow longer
and again I can journey north.

My Mirage

A few feet forward,
my mirage.
An oasis of my fertile mind.
Dreams devoid of camouflage.
Salvation yet to find.

Contentment
confuses reality.
My mirage –
delusion of my fantasy.

A manifest of what I want to be.
A simple nimble notion.
An illusion only I can see.
Protects me from implosion.
My mirage.

Let Me In

It's cold inside.
Let me in.
I won't overstay my welcome.
Let me in.
Take a chance, frigid heart.
Let me in.

I can melt your frosty nature.
Let me in.
Explore where our paths overlap.
Let me in.
Kindle a spark, a kiss in the dark.
Let me in.

Thaw the chill inside your words.
Let me in.
Feel my radiant love.
Let me in.
If just for a moment.
Let me in.

Are you cool or simply numb?
Let me in.
Melt some of the ice away.
Let me in.
Bring in the sun and
chase away winter forever.
Let me in.

High Fidelity

The door sounded like a violin
when you came creepin' and crawlin' in.
Then some drums and bass guitar,
tripped over Rover and broke a jar.
After two and look at you –
slurry speech, bloodshot eyes
directly from some scummy dive.
Don't mean to harp,
but accordion to my vibe,
you can't come home
rappin' such rapscallion.
I'll make it clarinet,
you cornet have xylophoned,
So wrong, you get the gong.
No triangle. No easy sax.
Find yourself another song.

George

Tell me what's in your heart, George.
You always do.
Even when I was small
you talked to me as if I had a brain.
And you listened
as if my thoughts meant something.
When I was very young,
I named a farm animal after you.
A great honor in our household.
And you took it in stride
with your warm humor.

We spoke of music together
and listened to Neil Young
on my small stereo.
You called "Hey Jude" the
best – and worst – song
the Beatles ever made.
And I was amazed
you knew them at all.
You spoke of Big Bands
that commanded the stage
without amplifiers.
And it opened a new door
to Sing Sing Sing and
Maynard Ferguson's bloody lips.
Your enthusiasm for music
and reel-to-reel tape recorders
held you in my high regard.
The sounds of "Sons of the Pioneers"
drifting upstairs in your
Torrance home,
serenading me to sleep
after a long day at Disneyland.

We talked of cameras
and 8mm home movies.
I worried about your ulcer
you battled as an
air traffic controller.
I couldn't even imagine
the responsibility that was
always on your shoulders.
And now, time has past,
with adult children of my own.
But you still listen
as if my thoughts mean something.
Thank you for always being
my favorite,
Uncle George.

Rise and Shine

Put one foot in front of another.
Don't beat around the bush.
Actions speak louder than words.
Pull instead of push.
The ball is in your court.
Don't bite off more than you can chew.
Take it all with a grain of salt.
When you tango, it takes two.
Hit the nail on the head.
Let the cat out of the bag.
Get it straight from the horse's mouth,
or you'll go from riches to rags.
Steal your own thunder.
Kill two birds with one stone.
Every cloud has a silver lining.
Do it today, don't postpone.
Make it your way or the highway.
Just know your own mind.
Follow the path of least resistance.
Leave closed doors behind.
Cross that bridge when you come to it.
Might be a blessing in disguise.
There's a method to your madness.
The cream will always rise.
Give it the benefit of the doubt.
Your guess is as good as mine.
Can't judge a book by its cover.
But don't cast pearls before swine.

Dog Years

Nearly a century in dog years,
the old hound only dreams
of chasing a ball as if it were a rabbit.
He loved that game. Cherished the chase.
Never tired of it. But now his bones
hurt when he runs. Or walks.
Age has muddled it all up
in a dawdly decline.
He didn't see it coming.

Sometimes in the morning
he'll race down the stairs,
prance like a pup
with a kick of exuberance –
until arthritis reminds him
those days have long past.

He goes on walks – a combination
of courage and conviction.
It's no coincidence he pees
on the same boulder every time.
It's his reminder to the world
he's still here. Still afoot.
Still the dog to deal with.

His old eyes tell his tales –
the memories when
life was all play and nothing hurt.
Or his grateful glance
thanking us for being his humans.

A day doesn't go by now that
he doesn't do something out of character
or pull some knucklehead stunt.
But the old pooch still
fetches his affection,
retrieves his devotion,
and galvanizes our hearts.

Forest Lodge

The crackling fire expires,
yields orange glowing embers –
a reminder of simmering summer
fading from September.

Goodbye
rhythm of crickets chirp.
So long, scents of cedar and pine.
Adieu to red mountain dirt –
all the trails I've left behind.

Tomorrow, the sea.
Deep waters of my soul.
Sirens sing soft melodies
luring me back to the shoal.

Pacify my traveler's heart.
Last day at forest lodge.
A piece remains as I part
and bid farewell, my bon voyage.

Empty Space

Satellite photos of Pluto
astound astrophysicists.
But it's the vastness
of space I find intriguing.
Earth is but a tiny
grain of sand in the
beach we call the universe.
Except the difference is
the distance between each pebble –
more like electrons in a molecule
supersized.

It's difficult to imagine
our place in the universe,
where light years and
our heavy years collide.
What's easier to imagine
is the empty space
between us.
So much in common
yet, so far apart.

It's not that we can't
be different.
We are, individually.
But our proximity
to each other
is more like the
planets and stars
than a handful of sand.
We create our own orbits.
And our own atmosphere.

Unlike the universe,
the course can be altered
and empty space reduced
between the planet
sitting next to you.
The vast majority of space
is empty.
It would be a shame
to live our lives the same way.

Domini's

I sit down in the 60's brown vinyl seat
and order the same sandwich I did
thirty years ago.
Roast beef with swiss on rye,
mustard only.
Tommy Lasorda was a regular once,
enjoying his usual salami sandwich.
They slice the bread, meats and cheese
when you order.
Fresh popcorn in chrome bowls,
complimentary.
Tropical wallpaper still on the wall,
with orange lattice bamboo art.
Order a whole sandwich and
take half home for another lunch.
They'll put more popcorn in your
orange and white striped take-out bag
and wrap your sandwich in foil.
This is not an ordinary lunch spot,
it's an institution since 1963.
Founder Al Domini died in 1999.
His credo, "Give 'em more
than they bargained for."
Son Joe now at the helm,
upholds the heritage.
Sure, my sandwich
has tripled in price
since my first soiree.
But to be able to
travel back in time
and still taste tradition
disguised as
roast beef and swiss –
a treasure for the palate –
a treat I will someday miss.

Metamorphosis

In my hand
a brown and black caterpillar.
Frightened, it rolls into
a fuzzy little ball
no bigger than a nickel.

Whispering to my soft clenched fist,
you'll soon become a butterfly.
With wings you'll soar
throughout the meadows –
throughout the sky.

Wary little caterpillar
no reason to be shy.
You'll turn yourself inside out;
digest all you've been about
before metamorphosis can apply.

No measure of mediocrity.
No treasure of circumstance.
No satiated desire
for fate to transpire ¬–
No shortcut in nature's dance.

Real change can never be
resolution for the half-hearted.
You must turn yourself inside out;
digest all you've been about
before the process is even started.

It takes total commitment –
with heart and soul in line –
to become the someone
you want to be
and leave the other behind.

Safe Harbor

Inside my soul is a little boy.
A tender heart. A sensitive spirit.
Curious. Creating questions.
Searching for answers.
Looking for love.

Through my many years I've built
protection for that innocent voice
from the dangers of the outside world.
What was once a simple shelter is now a fortress.
Shielded from enemy attacks.
Security from invaders and villains.

Yet, at what cost?
Somewhere in the bunker
is still that same little boy.
Craving to see the sun again.
Peeking out in fear
of his own destruction.

I had intended to safeguard my soul
but it ended up imprisoned instead.
Even as I attempt to tear down
some barricades of the bastion,
I've discovered they are harder
to remove than to create.

Inside my soul is a little boy.
Whom I can now visit more often
when I peel off the layers, one-by-one.
I know he's probably tougher than I thought.
And there never was a safe harbor.

I Light the Fuse

The spirit of the Fourth of July consumes me.

Children draw designs in the night sky
with sparklers
which they extinguish safely in a water bucket.
Adults prepare to drink in the fireworks
and set up the adirondacks while
adding bourbon to their coffee cups.
But it is I
who lights the fuse.
An explosion of sound and color,
like a cannon of kaleidoscopes.
The smell of burnt gunpowder.
The danger of a renegade rocket.
Each one spectacular.
Each one with more oohhs and aahhs
than the one before.
Finally, my match ignites
the grand finale –
a curtain of electric gold threads,
multi-colored missiles
and a twenty-one gun salute.

My head hits the pillow
screaming with temporary tinnitus
as I am serenaded to sleep
by the distant sounds of war
from overzealous night owls.

The Last Christmas

We were expecting
positive encouragement,
like we had gotten
so many times before.
Hope, especially
for the holiday season.
Three days before Christmas,
doctor told us
there was nothing more
he could do.
The cancer spread
into the only lung
that remained.
All the chemo,
surgery
and daily radiation
in vain.
"How long do I have left?" she asked
But the doctor couldn't
or wouldn't
answer.
It was the one time
we decided
to keep the news to ourselves.
Keep the secret inside
until the holidays were over.
Paste a Christmas smile
on our faces.
Decorate the tree.
Make frosted gingerbread stars.
Open presents with glee.
I may have drank
a little more wine than usual –
who could blame me?
On January second
I revealed the prognosis.
Added another patch
to her fentanyl regiment
for the pain.
And greeted the new year
with the apprehension of
knowing it was her last.

Same Old Song

I remember that sparkle in your eyes.
The beginning. Everything new.
Each detail, an adventure.
Each achievement, an accomplishment.
Like a yardstick on the wall,
where pencil marks date the growth spurts.
You looked up to me.
I was steadfast with vision.
And could see the future.

Then growing pains.
Emergencies. Fires extinguished.
Burning the midnight oil.
More people. More personalities.
Overcoming the tragic migrant accident.
Accolades for your sweat and hard work.
Meanwhile, I remained steadfast,
navigating the ship through the storm,
guiding it into harbor.
You began taking charge,
changing course without counsel.

Now you are taller than I.
And look down to me.
Head of the whole ball of wax.
Plowing through new horizons
like a bulldozer clearing land,
going in directions I don't understand.
You are conductor of this orchestra,
yet cannot hear my instrument.
I play a melody no longer in your music.
Now it's the same old song
I've heard many times before.
The one where I must leave
and reluctantly close the door.

High Bridge Park

Two miles from city center
at the confluence of the
Hangman and Spokane
lay the ghosts of our conscience.
Intruders hanged seventeen
Palouse natives there, forgotten
in a simple slip of history,
with the creek now called Latah
to erase embarrassment.

A nearby bog bore bones
bigger than boulders –
remains of a
prehistoric pachyderm
sat unbeknownst
until the same year
Rutherford Hayes
was elected president
without winning either
the electoral or popular vote.

The forest foliage swallows
streets and sidewalks of
an abandoned suburb
and a sanitarium long gone.
Nude sunbathing caused
caution among residents
and a pulled in a plethora
of peeping Toms.

Today's picnic
watches dog park canines
and frisbees fly on an
eighteen hole disc golf course.
High Bridge Park –
abandoned ancestoral
days of yore
and
forgotten mortalities.

My Favorite Pirate

Shipshape in my harbor.
Protected from attack.
Shielded from misfortune.
Sails still intact.
I want to head windward.
Cast off to points unknown.
Gain distance from the doldrums.
Avast abandon all alone.
Smuggle in my solitude.
Belay my bewitchment.
Safety in my Citadel.
A drifter in dissent.
That all changed when
you came aboard.
A shakedown from the start.
A buccaneering larceny –
the day you stole my heart.

Ides of My Essence

Middle age. Halfway there.
Further back today than forward.
Past greater than tomorrows.
Not sure it's what I ordered.

Time seems to pass faster now.
Or it is I who's become slower?
Is it the bane of human being
when we simply just get older?

The ides of my essence –
a reflection point indeed.
Another chapter. Turn the page.
Still bountiful words to read.

I look forward to my future days.
The ones not yet revealed.
Fate – a friendly compatriot.
Adventures far afield.

So long youthful exuberance.
Hello hindsight recollection.
Wisdom through enlightenment.
Discerning the right direction.

Insight is a precious rose,
grown from buds before it.
I'm more qualified than I used to be
to face the unforeseen and explore it.

Extra Credit

I'd like to do some extra credit
to balance out things to work on:
Like playing well with others.
Listen while others talk.
Learn I don't always get
to have my own way.
And not put things in my mouth.

May I please do extra credit
and advance my poor review?
I will listen and follow directions.
Sing a solo for the group.
Strive for good posture.
Keep my hands to myself.

My work is neat and orderly.
I like to share ideas.
Use my soft voice when
answering questions.
May I clean erasers at recess?
Or help pick up finger paints?
I need that extra credit to balance
the quizzes and complaints.

So, I'll do the extra job you ask
if it will benefit my report card.
But pretending I'm invisible
is a task not really very hard.

I Would Have Told Her

3:16am.
My attempt to
navigate back to sleep
was failing miserably.

In the silence of early morning
I was dying.
Uncomfortable.
Apprehensive.
My heart
under attack –
struggling to
keep blood pulsating
through my veins
despite a blocked artery.

"...forty percent mortality rate,"
echoed in her mind.
The doctor's last few words
while wheeling me away
into surgery.

I would have told her
odds are in our favor.
Maybe made a joke
to lighten the
swampy seriousness of it all.
"Don't worry, baby – I'll be fine.
Our future together bright."

But already sedated,
prepared for the procedure.
At the surgeon's mercy.
And the gentle hands of God.

She was there when I awoke in I.C.U.
The pain I must have put her through.

Gasping at Straws

Where's the roadmap?
Gentle guidance
that leads to
the right path,
the right choice,
the right place.

It's not always rosy.
Still headed in
the right direction?
Muddy puddles on
the way to pleasure?
Or jolted off-course
with wayward wander?

Orphan of abandon.
Streets without signs.
Life has no roadmap.
It's within you to define.

Listen to the wind.
It whispers
words to the wise.
Here your heart
beats true.
The compass inside
is you.

Earth Sojourned

It was our land before you.
This earth, this garden
we call our universe.
Where nature's bounty –
our food and shelter.
Tools and medicine.
Darkness and light.

For centuries
our bones buried
over those who passed.
Back into the earth,
reborn as rock, as water.
Until we come alive again
as bird in air.
Fish in sea.
Servant to soil.
Creature of countryside.

This was our path,
our cycle
before you came.
Then you tore
our earth open.
Carrying disease.
Forcing beliefs.
Planting machines
you call civilization.

We no longer
bury bones
upon the ancients.
No longer
feast off earth's riches
in communion
with its harmony.
Our salty tears
turn leaf's green to brown.
We fear
we'll remain
rock and water forever
when
Earth cannot save its soul.

The ancient anthems –
now sung too softly
for new generations.
So they sing a new song
without earth's harmonies.
Without its resonance.
Without its measure.
Now we must ascend
into your heaven.
Leave our earth
with solemn goodbye.

My Favorite Things

For nearly thirteen and a half minutes,
John Coltrane's rendition of
the Sound of Music classic
banished the banality
and reassembled its bones.

I've heard his version before.
So when I hit play
I already knew what I was getting into.
I needed a lift from a hot, tough day.
Coltrane was there
to cool it.

It's a meditation, really.
A mental massage.
A familiar melody
woven in an exotic fabric.
Notes on the page
and notes in the air.
Each a voice. Each an emotion.
Each an expression
understanding my angst
while answering with a lovely,
comfortable whisper
that all is well.

There's a certain peace
veering from the
melody awhile –
drifting like a conversation
from one related topic to another,
assuredly returning to
the subject at hand –
like a great inside story
hidden in the song.

When it ended
it was I who had changed,
not the music.
So I played it again.
It helped make me
indeed thankful
for my favorite things.

Lilith

Her mendacity was obvious,
but I was oblivious –
thinking what might transpire.
My senses knew
she was a toxic stew,
and I might burn
too close to her fire.
Yet I pursued her,
wooed her,
viewed her
with
irrational rapture.
Unaware she
purloined my heart
as I set about
hers to capture.

I can blame it on
her lavender scent
or lovely orchid eyes.
But truth
has no measure
in my malaise of madness,
which made me
so unwise.

Holiday Hubbub

'Tis the season of merriment.
'Tis the pageant of parties.
Calendar full of planned events.
Nog with a little Bacardi.

When I was younger
it was easy to embrace those days.
Fritter away my solace.
Get lost in the holiday haze.

Now, that I'm older
I seek refuge from the ruckus.
Steal back a bit of solitude
amid the holiday hocus pocus.

I'm thankful for friends and family.
They're a blessing, truth be told.
I love the time when we're together.
Traditions to uphold.

But I also like the quiet time
shared by me and you.
It helps me survive Christmas chaos
and the holiday hullabaloo.

Safe and Insane

They had a pitchfork fight in the barn.
Seemed a good idea at the time.
Like hitting blasting caps with a hammer
to see if they would explode.
These two brothers were kinfolk.
Tough as nails, those two.
One missing a finger, the other a toe.
When visiting, some things were taboo.
Like shooting targets with the 22.
Dad said no. Not safe. Not for you.
Find something else to do.
Tied some line at the end of a broom,
dug some worms, hiked the creek,
found a small pool, quiet and deep.
Caught six trout that day, all keepers.
Without kinfolk. Just my lonesome.
With an old broom instead of a gun.
The boys returned, showed me their targets.
Damn, it looked like fun.
Never got close to trouble
under my Father's watchful eyes.
I know he feared my safety.
For that I was penalized.

Merits of the Marshmallow

Someone called me
a marshmallow.
It irked me.
I felt shallow.
It meant I was soft.
Squishy. Pliable.
A coward
avoiding conflict.
Spineless;
Dreading encounters.

But consider the merits
of the marshmallow.
Drop one on the floor –
it will never shatter.
Insults simply bounce back off
and never really matter.
Marshmallows are honorable.
Predictable.
Palpable.
Palatable.
Dependable.
Digestible.
Delectable.

Perhaps it was a compliment
and I shouldn't have taken offense.
A marshmallow is no mockery.
In fact, it makes some sense.

Picket Fence Facsimile

From the outside
it looks ordinary.
We assume
what it means.
Middle class mustard
and salami sandwiches.
With an
artichoke inbetween.

Suburban swingset
in the backyard.
Roses by the gate.
The presence
of a quiet family.
Bicycles and
roller skates.

The appearance,
indeed innocence.
Wholesome
book of virtues.
Vanilla picket
fence insulation,
void of all taboos.

But facades
can be deceiving.
Perceptions
can be flawed.
Persuading eyes to
look the other way.
Gentle wink and then a nod.

What lurks inside
this picket fence?
Impossible
for us to see.
Weeping whispers
and muffled cries
reside in this facsimile.

Time Bandit

Woke up this morning
with a vivacious verve
to tackle the day, without delay
and pilfer the moments I deserve.

Looked at the clock
then strolled to the sidewalk.
Said "hi" to the neighbor,
picked up the paper –
the headline had me in shock!

'Man Steals Hours,' the headline read,
with my photo on the front page.
An exaggeration perhaps, true nonetheless,
and it put me in a bit of a rage.

How very strange, I thought to myself.
Is the world completely cuckoo?
Now I am wanted for borrowed time,
which I never knew was taboo.

Ignorance of law is no excuse,
that I realize –
but all that fear finally faded away,
when I opened up my eyes.

I lay there on my pillow
pondering the silly dream.
When I want a snack before I sleep
I think I'll cut out the ice cream.

"Time is like a handful of sand – the tighter you grasp it, the faster it runs through your fingers"
– Anonymous

A Flash in the Sky

I wasn't the only one who saw it.
That amazing flash in the sky.
Doubling in size.
Tripling in brightness.
Dwarfing the stars.
And then gone.
Sucked into
the obsidian cloak of night.

The news reported it was a star.
Exploding in 1776 –
the year
Washington crossed the Delaware.
And we were just seeing it now
because it took that long
for the light to travel to our eyes.

What I witnessed
happened 240 years ago.
But it occurred in the
moment I saw it as well.
It happened then
and happened now,
all at the same time.

As moments continue to
run through my fingers,
I wonder if someone
two and a half centuries from now
will see my brilliant flash of light
before it sinks into blackness.

Let it not take so long
for the light to travel to our eyes.
Time flies.
But we're the pilot.

Richie

Richie was my responsibility at the 1972 Los
Angeles Special Olympics. He was a handful –
a Down Syndrome kid of seventeen. And here
he was, with me, in a unfamiliar hotel room.
Afraid. Excited. Nervous. Without tools to
cope with such emotions. The plan, of course,
was to rest and get some sleep before the big
race tomorrow at Memorial Coliseum. Richie
was built like a runner. Lean. Slender. Strong.
And fast. In fact, he was prone to run away,
which is why I was assigned to him in the first
place. So we stuck together like glue, Richie and I.
Now it was time to sleep and Richie would have
none of it. He didn't have the ability to speak
in understandable words, so he communicated
in grunts and gestures. How can I calm him?
How can I get him to sleep so I can get some
shuteye myself? So, I invented the sleeping
game. We would both pretend to be asleep
and the first one to "wake up" would lose. This
became great fun for Richie, who put his head
under the covers and waited a couple minutes
until sitting straight up and loudly grunting
something that sounded like *"Morning!"* At least
he was laughing and smiling. I would remind him
that he lost the game and we would try again.
Eventually, after many games, he succumbed
to his exhaustion and fell asleep. The next day,
he was rested and in great spirits. I got him
to his events, one which he won a second
place medal. I lost touch with Richie after that.
I often wonder if he is still alive, since age
expectancy is usually around fifty years. But
more important, I wonder if he remembered
the thrill of getting a second place medal at
the award ceremony, in front of so many of
his peers. And I wonder if he ever played the
sleeping game with anyone else.

> your time young stallion
> shine in arena spotlight
> mine the memories

Judas was a Surgeon

Judas was a surgeon, Dad.
He was, you know –
it's obvious.
How else could
a simple operation
suddenly turn so serious?

Ten days in ICU.
Then baby steps
toward recovery.
Each day you must
grow stronger to
prohibit your own fatality.

This was not the plan,
I understand.
It wasn't what you were told.
Judas betrayed your
hopes and dreams
and left you bitter cold.

Recovery is a precarious path.
It feels like
your walk alone.
But you have many disciples, Dad.
More than you've even known.

It's the healing you must endure.
And the time
it takes to happen.
Build your strength.
Mend your wounds.
Starve discontent into famine.

Judas was your surgeon, Dad.
It's your resurrection now we pray –
to become the healthy man you were
and salute your eighty-fifth birthday.

Spirits of Siren

I first met him in line at orientation,
our eyes both following a pretty girl
as she sauntered out of the room.
We both said *"whoa!"* at the same time
and became fast friends in that moment.

His name was Wayne Boulac. Class clown.
Thespian. Energetic. Hairy. Had to shave
twice a day. Painted his fraternity room
ebony and lit it with black lights.
His white teeth phosphorescent.

We both had the future in front of us.
Him the actor. I the writer.
Nothing foreseen could get in our way.
But hidden rocks below can sink a ship.
Boulac heard a chorus I could not .

At first, the siren song was faint,
a gentle lure. A sweet melody.
He may have imbibed a bit more than I.
Neither one of us were saints.
And it was college, after all.

We went off to our adventures.
Degree in hand. Determined to
make our mark in the world.
His standup bombed in Vegas.
Returning home without as many dreams.

Siren's song kept calling.
Louder as each year went by.
Boulac eventually became a
stockboy at a supermarket.
And lived with his father.

He enjoyed his whiskey on the rocks.
The spirits of Siren kept pulling him closer.
And then, at 44, the day came when
he crashed upon the treacherous shore,
joining the Sirens who sang his song.

The Pomegranate Diet

I like fruit you can pick from trees
and bite into – like an apple.
But when my doctor ordered
I eat pomegranates,
I'd prefer he'd use a scalpel.

What scoundrel designed this silly fruit?
Is it one of nature's jokes?
A hard hide on the outside
that's simply asking for a poke.

It takes a knife to remove the skin –
a treacherous task indeed.
Not recommended for the faint of heart
if one really wants to succeed.

And finally the tenacious shell is shed -
teeming with seeds insurmountable.
Looking like an organ – bloody red.
A murder with no one accountable.

No wonder this is a diet food.
Seeds are gathered, one-by-one.
You simply just lose your appetite
before your meal is done.

Next time, do yourself a favor
when you're in the supermarket –
buy yourself a bag of grapes
and do the diet without it.

Picnic

Snow capped Cascades
frame the horizon
like ice cream sundaes
without the cherry.
Lavender lilacs
scent spring air
with sweet effervescence.
The day
demands
a picnic packed
to celebrate the
cusp of Summer's return.
Compulsory consciousness
required.

Abandon your cocoon.
Emerge as
the butterfly you are.
Spread your wings.
Flutter over flowers.
Dance in delight.
Inhale the
scents and sounds
of this moment,
this hour,
this day.
Surrender
tomorrow's worries
and yesterday's regrets.

Savor the taste of it.
Smell the lilacs once again.
Let the earth speak and
reveal its wisdom.
All you have to do
is listen.

Snake River Circus

The crowd
was ebullient –
buzzing with
anticipation.
A spectacular
solo stunt.
A skycycle leap
nearly a mile wide.
Could
Evel Knievel
make the jump?

It was hot that day
in Shoshone Falls,
amid the media storm.
At 3:36 in
the afternoon,
Evel was
ready to perform.

The steam-powered rocket
launched into the blue
with just one man aboard.
Crossing the canyon
to the other side
would be his true reward.

Alas, the chute
opened way too soon –
dealing the flight a blow.
Meagerly missing the canyon rim,
then down to
river bottom below.

Evel survived
this ballyhoo
without a benediction.
Could it all just have been
simply a slight of hand
on the same day
Gerald Ford pardoned Nixon?

Odonota

She prefers sapphires
over diamonds.
Silver rather than gold.
New Age instead
of rock and roll.
Scotch, more than beer, truth be told.

Not part of any colony.
Still searching
for her tribe.
Spirituality
versus religion.
Kindness undenied.

Lived already many lives.
Learned from those
less harried.
Prefers to remain
where her heart is true
in lieu of being married.

She shines a light
both out and in –
a beacon of her beauty.
Yet, can't see herself
through my own eyes –
often she disputes me.

With pigment and purpose
she paints my world
with captivating color.
Warms me with her
ardent amour.
Her bread to my butter.

Steady, sincere
and genuine –
a spattering of wit.
When yin finally
finds it's yang,
it elicits a perfect fit.

Piecing it Together

A thousand pieces sit in a box
patiently awaiting assembly.
Borders and corners first –
somehow all go together
by content, by color,
forming a frame for the rest that remain.
One by one. Snapping in place.
Landing a home from
suspension in space.

First time, the most arduous.
Exposing its clever secrets.
Decoding deceptive clues.
Forcing a piece that doesn't quite fit
until discovering the right one to use.
A blade of grass was really sky.
The red dot – not where I thought.
As the frame fills, fewer options
make it easier to find the spot.
Then, finally together.
Something to admire,
an accomplishment.
But eventually, the pieces
go back in the box
biding another attempt.

The old puzzle's been put together
many, many times.
Some pieces worn and torn.
A few missing and maligned.
I know there will come a day
when I must let the puzzle go.
Put it all behind.
It will leave but a memory preserved
before its sad decline.

Old Redmond

I remember Old Redmond of my youth
before Microsoft money and madness
modified the dull, sleepy little town
into a brand spankin' shiny New Redmond.

The Five and Dime was in the town center.
Saved my allowance for balsa wood gliders
and warm spanish peanuts in the rotating glass
case. My mother would buy a yard or two of
fabric and sew me a costume for the Bike Derby
parade. I was a clown with a cone shaped hat,
a painted sad face and a tin ratchet noisemaker
I spun around aimlessly while I walked
down main street with all the other kids.
Including my younger sister, who was a
ballerina. The town bank gave a silver dollar to
any kid in a costume when the parade was over.
And a box of cracker jacks.

They used to close the roads for bike races
around Lake Sammamish. We'd have our bikes
in town that day too, brightly decorated
with red, yellow, purple and blue crepe paper
weaved carefully in the spokes like a flower.

The fella who owned Farmer Jones Real Estate
played Santa at Christmas time, handing out
red net stockings full of fruit and candy
after the free movie and cartoons at the
Mond Theater. It was the same place we
welcomed back Jim Whittaker, the first
American to scale the summit of Mt Everest.
For a while, the theater had a buffalo in
a pen next door. Fed it corn husks
from our garden.

The drug store that developed black & white
film for my 616 box camera is no more.
They tore down the feed store and golf course
and built a Marriot and a Macy's. The bakery
where I discovered cream puffs now
replaced by a Whole Foods.

There is a place in my mind where Old Redmond
still exists. A place hidden from the hustle and
bustle.

Where youth could be spent all day long
on a single silver dollar.

The Strangest Everything

The book stood out somehow
on the library shelf,
compelling me to
place it in my hands.
A collection of poetry.
Odd. Not my cup of tea, usually.
My sophomore eyes
scan a few pages
and find the poem
"Coming Home on the 5:22"
I read:
"The rest I've been. The ape up in the tree.
The botanist below it. The moon boy
at every bodice. The missionary bee
sucking for souls. The gunner with his toy.
The stink of small ambitions. Party clown.
Professor Poop, pride of the noumenon."

Something clicked in my young mind.
I'm not sure I understood it,
but I loved it. The way the words
were put together. The attitude.
The alliteration. I heard the music.
This single poem from
such a happenstance
ignited the desire to
create my own wordly inventions.
The conception of my catalyst.

So thank you poet
John Ciardi.
For the inspiration
and the courage
to write your reality
so others could find their own.
The Strangest Everything
resided in my high school locker
three weeks overdue.
I smiled when I paid
the thirty-eight cent fine.

Spring Break

Can't fly to Cancun.
Can't go to the moon.
Can't travel anywhere exotic.
Spring break in my own backyard –
while taking antibiotics.

A trip downtown for ice cream.
I'll pretend to be a foreigner
with a fake French accent
choosing flavors to order.

Je veux du chocolat.
Je veux la cerise.
"Oui, I'm, how you say, from out of town.
A wonderful place to be."

May not have gone to Mexico –
just my home to convalesce.
But the look on that clerk's face,
an expression fuckin' priceless!

One More Day

I'm not the one who thinks about
sweet songs that fill the air.
I'm not the one who frets a lot
about what I'm goin' to wear.
I'm not the one who hears the news
and then head toward despair.
But I'm the one who wants to be
the future of your destiny –
anytime, anyplace, anywhere...

Don't care about the world's affairs,
don't care about the crime.
Don't care about the economy
or if a quarter's worth a dime.
Don't care about the price of gas
or if TV wastes my time –
But I'll always be there for you
a solid rock, with faith we face
any mountain we would climb...

Today is the day I'm living now,
because today you can't deny.
Today is when we make a choice
to be or just stand by.
I want to make the most of it
lift our dreams up to the sky –
I want you to be a part of me –
unlock the door, throw away the key
it's so easy if we try...

In our lives there'll come a time
when our days will have an end.
The time we have together now
is too precious to pretend –
I need the chance to say goodbye
with moments we can't spend.
Take each day and savor it –
there is no future to forget –
sometimes time is not your friend...

One more day, one more day –
Want to love into tomorrow.
One more day, just one more day –
Past is the best that I can borrow.
One more day, one more day –
I want to wake up and
be in the arms of you.

Trapped in Doldrums

Doldrums keep my ship still.
No wind to fill my sails.
No breath of heaven's relief.
Stagnation perched its tail.
I want to move on, move forward.
Make headway to the harbor.
But without task of helmsman,
I'm stuck here like a martyr.

A breeze will blow one day –
forecasted anticipation.
Perhaps if I imagine
somewhere else, someone else –
it'll assist my manifestation.
There are times I have foundered.
Times I've been marooned.
Times I know I should have left and
it wouldn't have been too soon.

Maybe it was mixed messages.
Too much introspection.
Perhaps I should have nixed it
and looked for new directions.
Doldrums keep my ship still
through no fault but my own.
Sometimes one gets the oars out
and moves ahead alone.

Burial of His Father
on His Third Birthday

John John saluting his
father's casket, Jacqueline
draped in mourning veil.
Little daughter Caroline
at her side, standing with
Bobby, Teddy and
Peter Lawford.

Black and white image,
burnt directly into my retinas,
forever laced with
sadness and confusion.

I was ill the day he was shot.
On the couch. Watching drama unfold.
News bulletins bully away
regular programming.
Commentators repeat
the little they knew
over and over
like haunting echos
of a round sung
without a melody.

Four days later,
a funeral at
St. Mathew's Cathedral.
175 million people
watched on their
"idiot boxes" –
a term I learned
from my grandfather.

A nation striving
to make sense of it all.
The loss so sudden,
so unexpected.
Looking for answers
where there were none.
Small wonder, some of us,
began asking questions.

Trouble with Fire

A bow and arrow seems like
an innocent enough play toy
for a child of eleven.
But I was the oldest,
which means I was the ringleader,
the one parents trusted and
the devil who was the most fun
when the cousins came over.
We broke an arrow while shooting
at a hay bale target. At the tip.
So the next adventure was to fix the arrow.
We all piled into the garage where
I put the metal tip of the arrow into the vice.
I first tried chipping the wood out of the tip,
but it was too slow and difficult. Then tried
drilling the broken wood out of the metal.
Neither fit the patience of an eleven year old.
Then, we saw the gas. Lawnmower gas.
Small amount in a paper cup.
It would simply burn the wood out of the tip
and we could unite it with the arrow again,
slightly shorter than before.
Just a little gas. Some left in the cup.
One of the cousins lit the match and startled
us all – the vice on fire, the flaming cup gas
flying out of my hand, into the air and
onto the left ear of my cousin Bobby.
I smothered the flames with old t-shirts
my father used as rags. We cleaned the
damage up so it looked like it never happened.
But Bobby's ear was red.
Just like a sunburn, I said to him.
None of the kids wanted to squeal.
All feared to fess up and get in trouble.
So Bobby wore his light windbreaker hood
from that moment on until they all
went home hours later.

Turned out is was a second degree burn that
required a skin graft. *Oh God, a skin graft!*
I found all this out the following weekend
when the cousins returned to visit.
I was prepared to face the worst.
Getting grounded. No allowance. Extra chores.
Early bedtime. Maybe a whippin'.
My parents, curious about Bobby's bandaged
ear, were told he accidentally burned himself
by my Aunt Eilene, Bobby's mother.
Wait a second, the story changed?
No punishment?
We took a walk, Aunt Eilene and I,
in the early part of the day.
In between coffee and cards, before dinner.
Calmly, she explained her disappointment in me.
The oldest of the cousin clan. The boy scout.
She detailed the horror of discovering what
had happened to her youngest son.
The expense of the emergency room.
Possibilities of permanent damage.
No excuse, she was right.
I apologized, of course. With tears. But it
seemed pale compared to the catastrophe
emerged from the fiery accident the week
before.
"I'm not going to tell your parents," she said.
"This is your lesson alone. Your burden to bear."

We walked back with painted smiles and
my ascension into adulthood. It was kept
secret until she died forty years later.
The truth came bubbling forth from
Bobby and his twin sister's lips
to my parents' ears at her wake.

The Earth is Flat

I once heard the story
about the earth being flat.
Sail into the sunset,
fall off and that was that.
It was truth for centuries
'til someone questioned it.
Maybe not a pancake
but an orb, a globe, a planet.

So the sun doesn't sink into the ocean.
But that's exactly what I see.
Everything in my myopic world
orbits and revolves around me.
I'm the center of the universe.
The star some call the sun.
The leading role in my own film.
The sheriff with his gun.

Perched from my perspective
I see what's in my sight.
My vision of the world.
My perception of what is right.
The things I hear, the things I touch
are all part of how I feel.
It's hard to imagine a cosmos
where my presence is surreal.

I know there's a larger world
that's stranger than I imagine.
One with a peculiar point of view.
One where I'm not the captain.
But how do we make that journey
where familiar can collapse?
Perhaps it's the fuel of faith that
propels the earth from being flat.

The Old Red Barn

I remember
the old red barn
at my grandparents home.
Climbing hay bales.
Making forts
and tunnels.

The calf with two heads
was born there.
Don't recall how
long it lived.
But it revealed even nature
makes mistakes sometimes.

My grandmother fed
her feral cats oatmeal
every morning.
They always thought the barn
was a good place
to have kittens.

It was a sad day
when they sold the farm
to the builders
of a housing development.
It rained during the estate sale
and the barn provided shelter.

I said goodbye
to the old red barn.
Goodbye to my
playful childhood memories.
It's gone now. All that remains
are images in my mind.

Those are the things
they can't tear down. Or build over.
I remember
the old red barn.
The perfect place
for hide and seek.

Never Go to Bed Hungry

I dreamt I was in a restaurant
that featured native foods.
Honey from the local bees
tubers in their stew.
A savory menu, yes indeed –
a decent place to dine.
But when I asked,
"Where's the meat?"
all they had was swine.
No cluck, no moo,
no clams or crab at all.
What kind of place
puts only pig on plates?
I couldn't believe their gall.
Then found another restaurant
just a little later.
Bagpipes in the background,
plaid kilt on the waiter.
Seemed to have a Scottish flair,
but I don't know how to say this...
To my horror, the menu read,
"Hello to All Things Haggis."

Time to Leave

The old maple
grew its green clothes
in April –
an umbrella
for Missy the horse
during spring rains
and shade
all hot summer long.
But now, late October
it's time to leave.
As its suit colors change
to gold, orange and red.
Green leaves
now just a memory.
The tree begins to shed
its threads
one by one –
assisted by
Autumn gusts
and crisp cold nights.
Time to
put Summer away.
A striptease until
the branches bare all.
A time for dormancy.
A time for rest.
A quietness ready
for a barren winter.
And cold
down to the bones.
Unlike house guests,
a dead-end job
or a relationship
spiraling downward,
it's always known
when it's
time to leave.
We all could be so lucky.

Time and Temperature

My first real job out of college.
The big time. 750 employees.
Inventors of the time and
temperature sign –
installed at six thousand
financial institutions.

10:36 and 72 degrees
were the company trademark,
supposedly the ideal moment –
the perfect warmth.

Hired as an Assistant Copywriter.
My office – a converted supply closet
with no windows. Secretaries
had to walk further for pencils
and white-out. They were surly
to my presence.

Two months since my hire,
the supervisor asked to see me
privately. At 10:36 in the morning.
He closed the door. It was
much cooler than 72 degrees.
He said,
my employment may have been premature.
So don't do something stupid
like buy a house.

Too late, I said.
We put money down last weekend.
He stared at me for a full moment,
with enormous angst in his eyes –
mumbled something and told me
to go back to work.

My first taste of the corporate world.
Certainly not my last. And although the
time and temperature wasn't always ideal,
I remained in the supply closet
and picked up my check for the next five years.

Saved your Home

We saved your home
from forest fire.
The rest were not so lucky.
Your dwelling stands.
Like an oasis, with cinders.
Miles of dead
and blackness –
your new
scenic passage.
Dank dark stench
of burn and smoke
will dissipate
in years forward.
Neighbors gone.
An eerie quietness.
You'll have to drive further
for groceries now.
And your panorama
isn't what it used to be.

But we saved your home
from forest fire.
The rest were not so lucky.

Two Valentines

Fifty-five trips
around the sun –
the 14th of February
was her birthday.
Born with a tiny
heart on her nose,
her auburn curls
captured mine
quite young.

She gave me two children
during our thirty four years –
a small piece of her
living on and
loving on –
despite the cancer
that stole her away.

I always thought
I would be lonely
on Valentine's Day –
but I see
so much
of her
in you.

Both Aquarius.
Hair of red.
The kindness
you impart.
And perhaps
the most
important thing –
loving me
within your heart.

Looking toward
our later years
with hope, with joy
with trust.
Making memories
with my best friend –
A new chapter.
A new start.

There will always be
a piece of me
who recalls what
Valentine's Day
implies.
Time is a part
of my history.
A farewell.
A good-bye.

But you are now
my Valentine
and the day
is our affair.
Your love
somehow
shares her spirit
And makes
being together
remarkable
and rare.

Where are you Carol Morrison?

There was a time
before I knew you –
an unhappy stranger,
a runaway.
Mad at your mother
in another relationship
with a new baby.

*Where are you
Carol Morrison?*

You lived with us
for eight months.
Attended high school
as a sophomore.
A foster kid perhaps,
but I called you
my older sister.

*Where are you
Carol Morrison?*

It was nice not
being the oldest –
for once.
Encouraging me to get the
Charles Atlas bodybuilding workout
from a page in my comic book
by giving me the dime.

*Where are you
Carol Morrison?*

Dancing to
your records, the 45's,
I learned the mashed potato
and the peppermint twist from you
and the difference between
Chubby Checker and Fats Domino.

Where are you
Carol Morrison?

Peering through the
Spiegel catalog together,
page by page,
asking me which women
I liked best.
Even at ten, it appears
I favored redheads.

Where are you
Carol Morrison?

Then, one day
you were gone.
Back to your mother,
somehow making peace with it.
You said we'd write.
And call.
But of course we never did.

Where are you
Carol Morrison?

I was back to
being the oldest, again.
More than that, though,
I learned what it was like
to have an older sister.
Too bad you couldn't stay longer.
I was just getting used to you.

Where are you today
Carol Morrison?

Just a Dream

Perhaps it was the kidney pie
or the last gasp of Absolute.
Something sent my mind far away
without a parachute.

It came on quite suddenly after
the eyes closed in my head.
Was it a dream or a different dimension?
Did the clock strike thirteen instead?

I was with the King in Africa –
It was hot and I was sweaty.
There were giraffes and lions and wildebeast
on the plains of Serengeti.

I was riding a baby elephant
on this strange Swahili safari.
We were hunting with spears and blowguns
and drinking dark Bacardi.

We weren't after wild game at all –
much to my surprise,
but numerals that had hands and feet –
Threes and Fours and Fives.

Our catch bag was not complete
until the numbers totaled ten –
I'm sure there was a profound reason,
but for what I can't portend.

I was working on my taxes
before this dream took place.
Perhaps a reason to hunt integers
is still something I must face.

My bag was full of numbers,
my gut was full of rum.
I awoke with a shot of adrenaline.
Back to reality I succumb.

A dream is just a dream.
But is it really all it is?
Transport to a world unknown.
An adventure of abyss.

When I Write

When I write, I put one word
in front of another.
Just like anyone, I suppose.
But it's also my canvas
where painted words are
brush strokes I compose.
I have all the tools I need
to craft something worthwhile.
The only thing that remains
is doubt.
Fear I'll create something ordinary.
Dismay in the way it turns out.
It happens when I type the first letter.
And the last punctuation mark.
Is it good enough to
stand upright on its own?
Is it stale or is it smart?
Will it endure in someone's heart
as it has in mine?
Or will it slip silently away –
at its best be
beleagueredly benign?
When I write, I try to put
doubt away for a while.
Cage it from my muted muse.
Protect it like a child.
And then maybe,
just maybe,
a phoenix will manifest.
One that will rise above
the crest of my distress.

Challenger

News Item:
January 28 marks three decades since
the space shuttle Challenger disaster
claimed the lives of its entire crew.

I was a space nut. In the early days of
the Mercury space missions, up at 4am,
tuned to the black and white TV screen.
T-minus 83 minutes and counting.
Bright-eyed eight year old.
It seemed like the most important thing
happening in the universe.
Acutely aware history was in the making.
And the science behind it all,
blazing new frontiers!
I groaned at the flight delays.
Sweated every lift-off.
Panicked when the mission was cut short.
Celebrated the splashdowns.
But after the first moon landing,
my interest faded into a *"been there, done that."*
Still curious, I suppose, but not nearly as
enthralled as I once was.

Then, seven astronauts gone.
At 32, I felt the surge of space-aged angst
running through the veins of my youth.
My brother-in-law Dick was laying tile in
our bathroom, beat-up boombox radio playing
sad, tears in your beer country songs.
He heard the news report and I turned on the
TV. We watched the unbelievable video
coverage of the explosion repeated over and over.
In living color. Speculation the crew might have
survived lasted several hours.

Two years went by before NASA tried again.
The victory was a footnote.
I didn't care like I used to anymore.
But glad no one died.

Welcome to the CIA

You can't just ask, you know.
It has to be clandestine.
A covert fundamental,
like secretly
taking your medicine.

It's all quite hush-hush.
Flair for the dramatic.
A world of secrets.
A life of lies.
Panacea for the panic.

We collect intelligence.
Wallow in self-importance.
Missions for the President.
Elusive whispers to the military
and abiding law enforcement.

Core values keep us ethical.
We collaborate with our cranium.
Just don't blame us when
your brave soldiers return
pushing up geraniums.

A Bitter Pit

Inside the luscious, tasty fruit
a bitter pit indeed.
Yet, tossed to disregard,
it becomes a growing seed.

Born a single sprout,
thrives at nature's mercy.
Too hot the sun, too dry a drought.
Roots acutely thirsty.

Rains finally come.
Replenish the hydration.
A pleasant plasma, a joyous juice,
organic exclamation.

Now that bitter pit
bears its own fruit as a tree.
Ascended from abandonment,
leaves sweet possibilities.

Winter Adieu

Spring awakens
life dormant –
dozing under
winter's blanket.
Sprouts squint shyly
as if
the sun's too bright
to rouse and embrace
early morning light.

Nature's instinct.
Urge to mate.
Proliferate.
Every breed
has its burlesque.
Fruitful fertility.
Eggs in a nest.
Spring beacons
its time sojourned.
Another beginning.
A bud. A birth.
A new leaf turned.

Fresh coat of paint.
Clean cobwebs
from the corners.
Hoe the garden.
Sow the seeds.
Weather's getting warmer.
Time to emerge from
slumber's cocoon.
Throw away
dank brown and gray.
Color's all a bloom!

Strumpet Tremolo

She was sleek
as a salamander.
Gentle as a rose.
Nubile as
the day is long.
A smile,
well composed.

Born from
dubious origin.
Orphaned early on.
Stunted roots
and cold stone soup.
A pauper
and a pawn.

The streets were
her sanctuary.
An asylum for her soul.
She learned fast
to win men's favor.
Their hearts,
she simply stole.

Her sensual
maneuvers
made it possible to leave.
She ascended
from the abyss and
found a way to breathe.

We're always quick to
criticize others
to whom we don't relate.
The shortest path
between two lines
is never really straight.

The Paper Mill

Sublime panorama,
the Columbia River Gorge.
Extraordinary natural majesty.
The paper mill is present still –
an environmental catastrophe.
Clear cut forests
from those before us.
Scuffed and blemished
earth's thin skin.
Dead fish by the thousands –
an accidental mill excursion.
Swears
it won't happen again.
Sore throat every morning
inhaling invisible
sulfur dioxide and
hydrogen sulfide –
pollution one can't see.
Desecration of
our air purity.
A miasma of misery.

Ambidextrous

Some people use
their left brain,
others use their right.
To be both creative and logical
can be a real plight.
Most use one side or another
but that theory I revoke.
I say if one side of my brain's asleep
it's damn time it awoke.
It might take some discipline.
It make take some practice.
But it makes no sense to be maudlin
or pretend its completely hapless.
I want my brain not to strain
on cognitive calculation.
Yet, I don't want to lose my muse
or my holistic imagination.
I don't want to favor one or the other
but use both to my potential.
I know there's a way to discover
what I consider essential.
A joining of the hemispheres.
A sense of self robust.
When encompassing the task of two
my brain becomes ambidextrous.

When Angels Laugh

A Cougar game, in Pullman.
Took the small town road.
Autumn smelled of potpourri –
Leaf colors set to explode.

Pregame function with VIPs
Scotch whiskey on the rocks.
Found our seats with surprising ease.
Hid the flask from the stadium cops.

I remember the game at halftime.
Then things got sort of blurry.
Our team, two touchdowns behind.
They always *"coug it"* early.

Suddenly in the parking lot.
The football game was over.
Took off for a dinner spot.
Should have had a chauffeur.

Ended up in a country bar.
A bad place to sober up.
Broasted chicken and cigars.
We were all a little nuts.

Don said something snide.
Sue was quick to counter.
Threw her thigh of chicken fried
onto the famed photographer.

Bar brawl meant time to leave.
Locals got in the scuttle.
Exiting was a duck and weave
Fly the coop, run from the rubble.

Don't recall when we got home
or exactly how for that matter.
But I do remember the chicken thrown
made Don madder than a hatter..

The Path

I am the path
guiding you
to reach for your intent,
I am the voice speaking –
saying what you meant.
I am a ticking clock
making moments
never spent.
I am tears
softly shed
in times of your lament.

I am the whisper you hear
when anger
overcomes reason.
I am a lighthouse flame
when you're
searching for a beacon.
I am hope
and a friendly harbor
when your courage weakens.
When nothing seems
to make sense sometimes,
I bring color to your cohesion.

I am the soul inside.
The spark that
will survive.
The spirit that
moves on forward –
after your body's died.

Some say
we're inseparable,
but that's not always true.
You may choose
to turn a deaf ear –
but I'll always listen to you.

With a Whistle, Whiskey and Why

Sounds like a country song,
like lassoin' the open sky,
get along little doggies, one by one.
With a whistle, whiskey and why.

Broke my heart, little darlin'.
You were my sunshine, apple pie.
I'm bleedin' Red River Valley.
With a whistle, whiskey and why.

Saw the storm a ridin' in.
No way to say goodbye.
All I've left is hat and horse
and a whistle, whiskey and why.

Clementine, you were so fine.
My heart's been stolen blind.
But you couldn't steal my memories
and my whistle, whiskey and why.

Took a bath for you once a week.
With suds in ample supply.
Now I only soak my sorrows
with a whistle, whiskey and why.

Don't let your babies grow up to be Cowboys.
Laredo lonesome, filly on the fly.
Spend time dreamin' of better days
with a whistle, whiskey and why.

Green Beans

We'd have three or four rows
of green beans in the garden.
Mom would hand us buckets
on a bright sunny day
and say, *"fill 'em up."*
Play would have to wait
until the chore was done.
But even after we picked 'em
the torture wasn't over.
Later, sometimes while watching TV,
the buckets came out again.
Beans had to be trimmed.
So we'd all take our piles
and remove the tips
over the spread-out newspapers.
We usually did enough for
at least one batch for Mom to can.
Then the jars would be stored
downstairs, awaiting dinners
when the garden was spent.
I didn't like green beans.
But they were the go-to
vegetable of choice for family dinners.
I ate them, grudgingly.
They were my sister's favorite.
Which didn't make me like
my sister any better either.
When I did get a choice,
it would be corn or peas.

Today, I've made my peace
with green beans. I like them
steamed rather than boiled.
French cut if possible.
As long as I don't have to pick 'em
and remove the tips.

Soft Landing

There once
was a man
who fell from the sky
but didn't die.
He made a soft landing.

Out of an
airplane.
Without a parachute.
Without a net below.
It's not hard
to imagine
how he felt
as he fell
through the air.
Four thousand feet to go.

My life is over.
My time is done.
There's no escape
from this one.
No place to hide.
No place to run.
Every second
the ground
gets closer.
Every second
is closer to over.
A little prayer
as he made the plunge.

Some say
it was a miracle.
Others thought it magic.
Unlikely as it may have been
he walked away from tragic.

Choice

A fork in the road –
moment of indecision.
No way to forebode
which path could envision.

One could lead to riches
far beyond all fantasy –
and grant all the wishes –
jewels of marvelous majesty.

The other – treacherous.
With nothing to reward.
Twist and turns dangerous.
Dead end dread explored.

The right choice, the toss of coin.
The wrong, oh what a pity.
The fate of future purloined
from happenstance, quite giddy.

Life choices happen everyday
without such somber origin –
but the path chosen interplays
and weaves it's own proportion.

Naked Bird

There it stood.
Naked as a jaybird.
But it was a turkey instead.
I had taken it out of the oven early –
just enough time to let it set
and cool enough for carving.
I went to the garage
and was gone for only five minutes.
In that time, Mom stripped it.
That savory turkey skin
I had been dreaming about for hours
as the scent of the bird
loomed in the kitchen
and tortured my taste buds.
Now it sat naked, ready for the knife.
I was irate. *"Why? Why? Why?"* I screamed.
"Where in the hell did the skin go?"
"It's not good for you," Mom replied,
"You shouldn't eat it."
Furious. I couldn't forgive her that day.

But now, years later,
I think back to that naked bird
and rewind the day over.
I wish I would have laughed
at that naked bird
and enjoyed Thanksgiving in better humor.
Mom's gone now, but I still think of her
every time Donna strips rotisserie chicken
I bring home from the store.
Mom was right, of course.
It just took me longer
to join the poultry skin strip club.
Where I'm now a lifetime member.

Morning, Without You

I found a long red hair on the counter today
and I missed you.
You weren't next to me in bed
when I awoke at daylight.
There was no aroma of coffee
because you're the one who makes it –
fuel for your daily jumpstart.
But most of all,
I didn't hear about your dreams –
ignition for our morning conversations.
The house is quieter when you are away.
I'm left with my thoughts swirling
or talking to the cat –
always a very short conversation.
I love beginning my day with you
and the times I don't
leave a vacancy and a vacuum
like a recipe lacking primary ingredients.
I like it better when we're together
than when we're apart.
And not just in the morning.

The Next Step

Don't forsake me, father.
Like an arrow, I am true,
aimed at assisting souls
who can no longer
help themselves through.

I am the mine's canary.
A gauge to guide the way
to fresh air
and present dangers
of the toxic here today.

You carved me from granite,
so I would be your rock.
To trust me in the tough times.
To help remember
what you forgot.

I share your tears and laughter.
I cannot feel your pain.
Or what it must be like
to now live in a foreign land
and hope it's all the same.

So let me lead, my father.
I will get you to the light.
Old ways are not
always the best ways
to separate wrong from right...

Please, don't fight me, father.
I am here for you.
Let's leave behind
some of your sadness
and your self-destruction, too.

Don't forsake me, father.
Like an arrow, I am true.
I will not guide you wrong.
Let me pilot a soft landing.
A gentle rendezvous.

Four Agreements

Life is just four agreements
It's simple when you know.
It's not all that complicated –
It's easy to let it flow.
You can make it tougher
and fill your heart with pain,
but following four basic rules
will free you from the chains.

Be true to you, say what you mean
especially to yourself.
Your integrity means everything –
your heart, your home, your health.
Always be impeccable
your words should speak the truth –
blend them with the power of love,
you don't need further proof.

It can't hurt your feelings
when it doesn't hurt your heart.
Just don't take it personally,
and suffering never starts.
Use your armor, protect yourself,
hassles gone from anyone else –
The things that others say or do
is up to them, not up to you –

Don't assume what you might think,
it's probably not the case.
If you suspect or speculate,
your mind's in the wrong place.
Ask if you have a question,
express what you want to say.
Just don't make assumptions –
they always get in the way.

The easiest one of all
may be the hardest one to do.
Just do your best, and all the rest
will make your life more true.
No self doubt, no regret
are bonus complements.
Do your best, it sets you free,
there's nothing to prevent.

The Me I Thought I'd Be

I imagined, in my youth –
a disc jockey radio star.
Perhaps a TV News announcer.
A reporter ala Woodward/Bernstein,
purveyor of the Fourth Estate.
Or a poet.
In college, I set out for the stars.
Climbed the stairways to
reach those lofty ambitions –
tasted some of those aspirations,
then setting them aside for
slightly more practical ventures.
Endeavors that would
pay the rent. The heat.
And the expense of children.
That worked for only a while.
My penchant for independence
found me out on my own,
mining a livelihood
writing for others.

Now I'm done with that.
I can write for myself again.
Long ago.
The me I thought I'd be.
A poet.

www.ingramcontent.com/pod-product-compliance
Lightning Source LLC
LaVergne TN
LVHW011335080426
835513LV00006B/359